THE LAWBOOK EXCHANGE, LTD.

Foundations of the American Law of Lawyering Series

GENERAL EDITOR: Michael H. Hoeflich

"You Should Not"

A Book for Lawyers, Old and Young,
Containing the Elements of Legal Ethics

Foundations of the
American Law of Lawyering

The Foundations of the American Law of Lawyering Series presents reprints of works published in the nineteenth and early twentieth century that illuminate the ethical origins of the heritage of the legal profession in the United States.

"YOU SHOULD NOT."

A BOOK FOR LAWYERS, OLD AND YOUNG,

CONTAINING

THE ELEMENTS OF LEGAL ETHICS.

By SAMUEL H. WANDELL,

COUNSELLOR AT LAW, OF THE NEW YORK BAR,

Author of "The Law of Inns, Hotels and Boarding Houses," "The Law
Relating to Disposition of Decedents' Real Estate,"
"The Law of the Theatre," etc.

" I charge you by the law,
Whereof you are a well-deserving pillar."
—Merchant of Venice, Act IV, Scene 1.

With a new introduction by
Michael H. Hoeflich
John H. & John M. Kane Professor of Law,
University of Kansas School of Law

THE LAWBOOK EXCHANGE, LTD.
Clark, New Jersey

ISBN 978-1-61619-455-0 (hardcover)
ISBN 978-1-61619-460-4 (paperback)

Lawbook Exchange edition 2014

The quality of this reprint is equivalent to the quality of the original work.

THE LAWBOOK EXCHANGE, LTD.
33 Terminal Avenue
Clark, New Jersey 07066-1321

*Please see our website for a selection of our other publications
and fine facsimile reprints of classic works of legal history:*
www.lawbookexchange.com

Library of Congress Cataloging-in-Publication Data

Wandell, Samuel H. (Samuel Henry), 1860-1943.
  You should not, a book for lawyers, old and young, containing the
elements of legal ethics / by Samuel H. Wandell ; with a new introduction by Michael H. Hoeflich, John H. and John M. Kane Professor of Law
University of Kansas School of Law.
     pages cm
  Includes bibliographical references.
  ISBN 978-1-61619-455-0 (hardcover : alk. paper) -- ISBN 1-61619-455-
3 (hardcover : alk. paper)
  1. Legal ethics. I. Hoeflich, Michael H. II. Title.
  KF306.W27 2014
  174'.3--dc23   2014024004

Printed in the United States of America on acid-free paper

Introduction

🖙

Samuel Wandell, *You Should Not*
(1896)

Michael H. Hoeflich*

Samuel Wandell was a New York lawyer, judge, and prolific author both of law books as well as of biography and literary works. He was born in 1863 and died in 1943. His most celebrated book was his two volume biography of Aaron Burr written with Meade Minnergerode as well as a companion volume on materials related to Burr.[1] Amongst his other non-legal works was an historical volume, *Oliver Phelps*, a biography of Thomas Jefferson, and a play based on Thackeray's *Pendennis*.[2] His most important legal works were his *Law Relating to the Disposition of Decedent's Real Estate*, his *Law of Inns, Hotels and Boarding Houses*, *The Law of the Theatre*, *The Law in Relation to Public Contract Liens*, and the volume reprinted here, *"You Should Not," A Book for Lawyers, Old and Young, Containing the*

---

* John H. & John M. Kane Professor of Law, University of Kansas School of Law, 2014.
[1] S. Wandell & M. Minnegerode, *Aaron Burr* (N.Y., 1925); S. Wandell & M. Minnegerode, *Aaron Burr, A Bibliography...* (N.Y., 1925).
[2] S. Wandell, *Oliver Phelps* (Albany, 1941).

Elements *of Legal Ethics*, published in Albany, New York in 1896 when Wandell was still a relatively young lawyer.[3]

Background & Context

"*You Should Not*" was published at a critical moment in the history of the American legal profession and of legal ethics. Prior to the Civil War two major works on legal ethics appeared, David Hoffman's *Fifty Resolutions on Deportment* published as an appendix to the second edition of his *Introduction to Legal Studies*[4] and Judge George Sharswood's *Introduction to Legal Ethics*. Most modern scholars hold that these two works were the primary sources for legal ethics instruction in the antebellum period. In fact, lawyers could also gain insight into proper professional behavior through reading the many periodical pieces, including fiction about lawyers that were published, by attending public lectures given before bar associations, law schools, and other significant public events, or by hearing the eulogies delivered at the funerals of prominent lawyers.[5] Judge Sharswood's *Introduction* was derived from a course he taught at the University of Pennsylvania law school and legal ethics also were taught as part of other substantive courses at places like the Harvard Law School.

---

[3] S. Wandell, *The Law Relating to the Disposition of Decedent's Real Estate...* (N.Y., 1889); S. Wandell, *The Law of Inns, Hotels, and Boarding Houses* (Rochester, 1888); S. Wandell, *The Law of the Theatre...* (Albany, 1891); S. Wandell, *The Law in Relation to Public Contract Liens...* (N.Y., 1932); S. Wandell, *You Should Not* (Albany, 1896).

[4] D. Hoffman, *A Course of Legal Study* (2nd ed., Baltimore, 1836). This was first published as G. Sharswood, *A Compend of Lectures on the Aims and Duties of the Profession of Law Delivered Before the Law Class of the University of Pennsylvania* (Phila., 1854).

[5] See, M.H.Hoeflich, "Legal Ethics in the Nineteenth Century: the Other Traditon," *University of Kansas Law Review*, v. 47 (1999), pp. 763ff.

In addition, proper professional deportment certainly was one of the things that young lawyers were expected to learn by observation of other lawyers particularly during their apprenticeships, the dominant mode of legal education during the antebellum period.[6] What was absent during this period, however, were official codes of ethics, which did not appear until the Alabama Bar adopted its first code of legal ethics in 1887 and the American Bar Association followed with its first official Code in 1908.

One might well ask why there was so little attention paid to legal ethics among the numerous law books published in the antebellum period and why no formal codes of ethics were adopted by bar associations of the time. The answer to this question has been little explored in modern literature on legal ethics, but it is possible to suggest that the primary reason for the absence of more works on the subject was that the American Bar in the antebellum period was relatively small and that self-regulation through peer pressure was enough to maintain some degree of ethical standards. Certainly, there were instances of legal malpractice during the period, some of which found their way to trial.[7] There were also a number of notorious cases that led to both professional and public speculation as to the state of lawyers' ethics and morality. But, for the most part, lawyer behavior was unregulated and what writing appeared on the subject came from the urban legal elite.

The end of the Civil War brought massive changes to American society, changes which did not leave the legal profession untouched. Karen Haltunnen, in her brilliant

---

[6] On apprenticeship, see, eg, Paul H. Hamlin, *Legal Education in Colonial New York* (N.Y., 1939).

[7] See, for instance, W. Sampson, *A Report of the Case of George W. Niven...Accused of Malpractice*, with an introduction by M.H.Hoeflich (N.J., 2011).

analysis of post-Civil War America, *Confidence Men and Painted Women*, has shown that after the Civil War, Americans began to experience a widespread sense of social insecurity, a belief that they were no longer as safe or secure as they once had been in the halcyon days before the war.[8] One sees this insecurity and sense of danger in many of the books published in the second half of the nineteenth century, volumes with titles such as *Shams or Uncle Ben's Experiences with Hypocrites* and *Twenty Years of Hus'lin.*[9] This was a period in which middle class Americans experienced major financial crises, such as the Panic of 1873 which, in fact, lasted until 1879, massive stock manipulations exemplified by the activities of Jay Gould and Jim Fisk and other owners of the Erie Railroad and chronicled in Henry and Charles Francis Adams' *Chapters of Erie,*[10] and the great fires which destroyed much of Chicago and Boston in the early 1870s. It was also a period that saw massive demographic changes. Many Americans were beginning to move out of the countryside into the growing urban centers, a demographic shift that undermined the sense of community found in small town America. It was also a period that saw markedly increased immigration to the United States of Irish, Italian, and Eastern European Jewish populations with language, religion, customs and social practices quite different from those who had preceded them. And, of course, this was the period of the great migration westwards made possible by the transcontinental railroad and the growth of a national system of transportation, a phenomenon which meant that no town in America, no matter how small or remote could

---

[8] K. Haltunnen, *Confidence Men and Painted Women: A Study of Middle-Class Culture in America, 1830–1870* (1982).

[9] John S. Draper, *Shams or Uncle Ben's Experiences with Hypocrites* (Chicago, 1887); J.P. Johnston, *Twenty Years of Hus'ling* (Chicago, 1889).

[10] Henry Adams & Charkes Francis Adams, Jr., *Chapters of Erie and Other Essays* (Boston, 1871).

remain cut off from the changes sweeping the country.[11] All of these changes, social, demographic, financial, and legal meant that to most Americans the world was becoming a frightening place and life seemed far more insecure than it had once been.

The Profession After the Civil War

Not surprisingly, the vast changes that shook American society in the period after the Civil War also had a profound effect upon the legal profession. Perhaps, most important of these were the rise of major corporations, particularly the railroads and the change these wrought upon the legal profession throughout the United States.

The growth of railroads and the rise of the large corporations that owned and controlled them profoundly changed the nature of the American legal profession. Railroads needed lawyers to attend to the myriad legal tasks that were required for their maintenance and growth. In addition to contributing to the new specialty of corporate law, railroads in their early years were also extremely dangerous and did extensive damage both to property and to human life. This naturally led to an expansion in litigation against the railroads by those who suffered these injuries.[12] This new litigation against railroads led both to an expanded demand for legal services by the injured but also a stratification of the legal profession. Railroads tended to hire lawyers from the professional elite. These were men

------

[11] See, eg., C. Miner, *A Most Magnificent Machine: America Adopts the Railroad, 1825–1862* (Lawrence, KS., 2010); R. White, *The Transcontinentals and the Making of Modern America* (N.Y., 2011).
[12] On the impact of the coming of the railroads on law, see, R.S. Hunt, *The Impact of the Railroad on Wisconsin Law in the Nineteenth Century* (Madison, 1958); J.W. Ely, Jr., *Railroads and American Law* (Lawrence, KS., 2001).

whose loyalties lay with their corporate masters. Lawyers who sued railroads tended, for the most part, to come from the less elite strata of the Bar. Within a very short period this stratification between elite corporate lawyers and the lawyers who represented plaintiffs against the railroads became quite pronounced.

The legal elite who comprised the membership of the corporate Bar were also, in many cases, those who were educated in university-affiliated law schools[13] and the faculty at these schools tended to align themselves with this elite stratum of the Bar. The legal elite, also, not surprisingly, tended to be the lawyers who were instrumental in reviving bar associations and other professional legal groups. And, of course, for the most part this legal elite was composed almost exclusively of men whose families had been well established in the United States well before the waves of late nineteenth century immigration. Members of these immigrant groups were virtually excluded from the legal elite and, therefore, tended to become members of the plaintiff's Bar instead. Thus, the disdain felt by the elite corporate lawyers for the emerging plaintiff's Bar was, one might suggest, a disdain born out of loyalty to their corporate clients as well as the common prejudice against immigrants.

In addition to the stratification of the Bar brought about by the rise of a new "corporate America," lawyers also shared in the general feeling of financial, social, and cultural insecurity of the wider population in the post-Civil War period. This insecurity gave rise to a growing sense of nostalgia for an earlier period when there were fewer lawyers, a more localized Bar, and when the legal profession was more culturally homogeneous. Of course,

---

[13] See, M.H. Hoeflich, *The Gladsome Light of Jurisprudence. Learning the Law in England and the United States in the 19th Century* (Westport, CT., 1988), intro.

there had always been a tension between the organized, elite Bar and those who were labeled as "pettifoggers," but in the later nineteenth century, with the increasing urbanization of the Bar, the expansion of legal education into new forms, and the stratification discussed above, the legal elite not only began to feel more threatened by a new generation of "pettifoggers," but also began to take actions against those whom they felt were undeserving of Bar membership. These reformist activities took many forms, including increased efforts to impose "ethical" standards on all lawyers. These standards, of course, were the standards of the elite and, in many cases, made Bar membership and professional survival more difficult for the non-elite members of the Bar.[14]

These post-Civil War trends discussed above can be illustrated by the lives and writings of two elite lawyers of the time, Thomas Goode Jones of Alabama and Robert D. Coxe of Philadelphia.

Thomas Goode Jones was born in 1844 in Georgia to well-to-do parents.[15] He attended Virginia Military Institute until 1862 when he joined the Confederate Army serving under Stonewall Jackson. After the war he returned home, married, and began to farm. According to Paul M. Pruitt, Jr., he attempted to "live in[16] pre-war style," a hint, perhaps, of nostalgia for the antebellum era. He also began his legal career and was admitted to the Alabama Bar in 1868. His career as a lawyer and politician flourished after his admission. He became a prominent railroad lawyer, active in professional organizations including the Alabama State

---

[14] See, generally, C. Andrews, "Standards of Conduct For Lawyers: An 7800 Year Evolution," *SMU Law Review,* v.57, no. 4 (2004), pp. 1434ff.

[15] Biographical details are taken from Paul M. Pruitt, Jr., "Thomas Goode Jones: Personal Code of a Public Man," in *Gilded Age Legal Ethics: Essays on Thomas Goode Jones' 1887 Code* (Tuscaloosa, 2003).

[16] Ibid., p. 69.

Bar Association.[17] In 1884 he was elected to the Alabama Legislature and became Speaker of the House in 1886. In 1890 he was elected Governor. In 1901 he served as a delegate to the Alabama Constitutional Convention and in 1907 became a judge.[18]

In the 1880s Jones began to realize the need for a formal code of ethics for Alabama lawyers. This code, which he authored, was adopted by the Alabama State Bar Association on December 14, 1887.

Paul M. Pruitt, Jr. has observed that the:

> ..."law provided a system of belief in which Jones found roles consistent with his principles of honor... Jones was inclined to describe chivalrous rivalry as a component of civilized behavior... Jones was well aware that many lawyers of his day had no intention of engaging in fair combat if they could help it.[19]

Jones' nostalgia for the antebellum period when lawyers were, in theory, if not fact, gentlemen raised in the Southern cavalier tradition, moved him to believe in the necessity for ethical reform in the less refined, less gentlemanly post-war South. Additionally, his experiences as a railroad lawyer also made him realize that the elite Bar faced dangers both from its new corporate masters and from the new plaintiffs' attorneys who sought to defeat the railroads in court no matter the method necessary. Jones realized that corporations had far greater power over lawyers than more traditional clients, power so great that it could impinge upon lawyerly autonomy and coerce lawyers into taking actions they would otherwise consider impermissible.[20] As to the newly arising "plaintiffs' Bar," Jones realized that

---

[17] Ibid., p. 71.
[18] Ibid., pp. 82–89.
[19] Ibid., pp. 76–77.
[20] Ibid., pp. 58–59.

these lawyers, often ill-trained and economically and professionally at a distance from the elite members of the Bar, would often sacrifice honor and traditional ethics for a courtroom victory.[21] Thus, the need for some formal regulatory scheme applied to lawyers seemed clear to Jones and the other members of the legal elite.

Richard D. Coxe was born a world away from Thomas Jones in Philadelphia into a prosperous family. He was a successful lawyer and Bar leader. Among his professional achievements was his service as Secretary of the Law Academy of Philadelphia.[22] He is best remembered, however, for his *Legal Philadelphia* published in 1908.[23] While nominally a history of the Philadelphia Bar, the book is, in many respects, Coxe's memoir and is full not only of his reflections on prominent Philadelphia lawyers and judges but also of his nostalgia for an earlier era in the history of the legal profession. That nostalgia encompasses, among other things, a longing for a time when the behavior of lawyers, in Coxe's judgment, was superior to what it had become at the time he wrote the volume. Cox saw the decline in professional behavior as caused by several changes in the nature of legal education and legal practice. First, he bemoaned the increasing dominance of law schools as the primary method of educating lawyers. He longed for the day when young lawyers were trained by the apprenticeship model and spent time in the offices of senior, distinguished members of the Bar. He believed that apprenticeship and close contact with established lawyers not only taught the young the substance and practice of the law but also the principles of good professional character:

---

[21] Ibid., p.78.
[22] I. Hazelhurst, *A Memoir of the Late Hon. Peter McCall* (Philadelphia, 1881), p.3.
[23] Robert D. Coxe, *Legal Philadelphia* (Philadelphia, 1908).

Almost invariably, there was a daily affectionate intercourse between what was, really, a preceptor, and what were, really, pupils; of incalculable service in the development, formation, and perfection of the personal, not less than the professional character.[24]

Indeed, Coxe comments:

One indisputable fact, adverted to in no invidious sense, but which it may be fairly urged proves that the law-office was more successful than the law-school as an agent in maintaining a standard of conduct is this: the several individuals who have, of late years, been disbarred for unpardonable violations of professional ethics, were, without exception, the exclusive products of the law-school.[25]

Coxe also believed that standards of deportment at the Bar had declined because of the shift of legal practice from a small, geographically coherent, community to a more widespread area dominated not by small ground floor offices but by larger, multistory office buildings. In recalling the old "legal neighborhood" of Philadelphia and its effect upon the Bar, he commented:

It was a purely professional neighborhood; with no trace of the commercial or general business character in it. There must have been a subtle element in such a refined environment which favorably affected the professional standard of conduct. However keen the legal warfare waged by as able lawyers as ever practiced at the Philadelphia bar, in those modest, severely plain, and insignificant old court rooms, the mutual courtesy which was, with the rarest exceptions, the dominant note, found

---

[24] Ibid., p.11.
[25] Ibid., p.13.

pregnant germs in the superior air they were privileged
to breathe.[26]

You Should Not

"*You Should Not*" when viewed in its professional and
historical context may be seen as the attempt by a rising
lawyer who was a member of the legal elite to cope with the
many issues that he and his colleagues perceived to be
problematic in the profession. He was old enough to have
been trained by the antebellum legal elite in their values.
Living in New York during the last quarter of the
nineteenth century he would have seen the rapid growth of
the corporate Bar in reaction to the growth and spread of
industrial corporations centered in the city. New York, as
the endpoint of many European immigrants' journeys, was
the home to large immigrant populations and a concomitant
increase in immigrant lawyers needed to serve these
populations. The Bar, itself, was growing, even beyond
these men, simply to serve the vast numbers of new
inhabitants of the city. All of these factors would have
contributed to Wandell's perception that a guide to
"professional deportment" was necessary.

Wandell's new guide was far more than a treatise on
legal ethics. It was an attempt to provide new members of the
Bar with instructions not only as to their professional
responsibilities but, also, to help them understand how best
to fit into the culture of the Bar, at least as Wandell
understood it.

---

[26] Ibid., pp. 20–21.

Character & Deportment

No detail was too minor to be ignored in *"You Should Not."* The first chapter of the book on "Yourself in General" is a compendium of helpful hints on basic issues for the young lawyer. The advice begins with comments on a lawyer's proper appearance including that one's clothes should be clean and neat, but that the young attorney should not attempt to be a "dude."[27] So, too, should the young lawyer take care in the choice of his office location and understand that success at the Bar demands hard work, honesty, and humility.[28] Wandell cautions his readers that they must not become conceited and that they should "not devote your whole life to the abject service of Mammon." [29]A young lawyer should "combine caution, discretions, and good judgment with energy."[30]

In addition to paying close attention to the location of his office, the young lawyer is also advised to take care that it is clean and dust-free.[31] Equally important, the young lawyer should not allow his office to become an "open house for idlers or gossips."[32] A lawyer's office is a place for diligent and serious work, not for smoking and idle chatter.

On the subject of character, Wandell urges his readers not only ot be assiduous in their work but to study constantly, to learn about human nature [including the ability to "read character by physiognomy"][33] and about as many practical subjects as they possibly can. Including

---

[27] Op. Cit., n. 3, above, p. 1.
[28] Ibid., pp. 2–3.
[29] Ibid., p. 3.
[30] Ibid., p. 5.
[31] Ibid., p. 7.
[32] Ibid., p. 7.
[33] Ibid., p.14; see, also, M. Hoeflich, "Lawyers and the Science of Character," in *The Green Bag.*

agriculture, science, and engineering in order to prepare themselves for cross-examining witnesses in these varied fields.[34] He also cautions his readers to avoid procrastination in all of their endeavors.[35]

Wandell dedicates a full chapter to what he refers to as "morals." In this chapter he tells his readers that, above all, they must cultivate good morals in their personal lives as well as their professional lives and to develop good habits that he characterizes as the "corner-stones of character."[36] He stresses that "honesty is the best policy for a lawyer" and urges his readers to avoid dishonest acts and avoid "rogues and sharpers" as clients.[37] Wandell cautions that a lawyer "is a servant of the public" and that a lawyer "is dependent for his business and support upon the good opinion of his fellowmen."[38]

Legal Ethics

Throughout *"You Should Not"* Wandell comments on subjects of what today we would call legal ethics and professional responsibility. In much of what he says he echoes the earlier works of Hoffman and Sharswood, as well as those of other later writers on the subject.[39]

Chapter 4 is titled "Your Clients" and deals, in large part on how a lawyer should deal with his clients in an ethical manner. Then, as now, the lawyer-client relationship was viewed as central to any ethical scheme for lawyers. Wandell begins the chapter by telling the reader not to do

---

[34] Ibid., p. 15.
[35] Ibid., pp. 15–16.
[36] Ibid., p. 42.
[37] Ibid., p.43.
[38] Ibid., p.43.
[39] See, above, at p. 6.

business with a client.[40] He then moves on to advise his readers that they should not "provoke litigation" or advise a client to "commence litigation where the chances of defeat are almost certain" in order to earn a fee.[41]

Wandell also deals in this chapter with an issue that greatly concerned writers on legal ethics during the nineteenth century: whether a lawyer should represent a client whose cause was unjust.[42] His advice is simple and to the point:

> You should not take up every case that is offered you. Learn to discriminate in the selection of cases...Try to select clients who are worthy of legal assistance, who have right and justice on their side.[43]

Wandell also tells his readers that they should not collect funds on behalf of their clients and never "mingle it with [their] private funds" because "in a moment of weakness, you may yield to the temptation to use it temporarily."[44] This, states Wandell, "is like driving a nail into your professional coffin."[45]

On the subject of confidentiality of client information, Wandell is equally determined:

> You should not betray a confidence that is reposed in you as a lawyer...The law office should be as inviolate as the confessional.[46]

---

[40] Ibid., pp. 17–18.
[41] Ibid., pp. 18–19.
[42] See, M.Hoeflich "Legal Ethics in the Nineteenth Century: The Other Tradition," *University of Kansas Law Review.*
[43] Op. Cit., n. 47, above, p. 20.
[44] Ibid., p. 21.
[45] Ibid., p. 21.
[46] Ibid., p. 22.

Wandell, in the same chapter deals with potential conflicts of interest:

> Neither have you the right to engage in a case against one who has offered to employ you and who has consulted you. After a man has unbosomed himself to you in the sacred confidence that exists between the attorney and the client, it is little better than knavery to turn on him, and use the information so obtained to defeat his cause. Attorneys should conduct themselves that any one in need of advice may state their matters freely, without reserve, and know that the confidence will be respected.[47]

One other topic with which Wandell deals in this chapter is very much representative of changing law of the period. In the period after the Civil War the legislatures of many states, whose laws on divorce had become rather lax, decided to reverse direction and passed laws that permitted married couples to divorce only on proof of certain specified justifications, eg. infidelity. Although legislatures were seeking to limit the ability of couples to divorce, the demand for divorce did not lessen. As a result, many couples engaged in what came to be called "collusive divorce" in which one of the them (usually the husband) would arrange to be "discovered" in a compromising situation with a woman not his wife and then, the wife would sue for divorce on the basis of this "infidelity." Of course, all of this had been arranged in advance as had the financial terms of the divorce.[48] Such collusive divorces required lawyers who were willing to look the other way when reciting the facts to the court. Wandell disapproved of this practice and he instructed his readers to:

---

[47] Ibid., p. 23.
[48] See, L. Friedman, *A History of American Law*

> ...hesitate to pander to the base designs of some would-
> be client, who, having no legal grounds of action, desires
> to circumvent the law and defeat its provisions by
> artifice and fraud.[49]

In his chapter on fees, Wandell betrays a mindset at once modern, but, also very much that of the nineteenth century. Like modern rules of professional conduct, Wandell's advice to his readers is not to "fleece" his clients, but, rather, he cautions that a lawyer's fee should be "reasonable."[50] On the other hand, Wandell spends far more space in giving advice to his readers that they should seek retainers and charge fair value for their services. He cautions about becoming known as a "cheap lawyer." He also tells his readers that they should not sue clients for unpaid fees unless "the amount involved is large."[51] It is relatively easy to see in this advice the perspective of a member of the elite Bar and one who despised the "cheap lawyers" who sought to serve poor and often immigrant clients.

In his chapter on "Yourself in Court" Wandell emphasizes good grooming, being well-prepared, not overreaching on cross-examination and other similar matters of behavior. He does also deal with two issues that modern lawyers would consider to be matters of professional ethics. First, he cautions his readers not to "attempt to deceive the court, or mislead the judge."[52] His second piece of advice concerns what today we would refer to as inadvertent disclosure of documents [as well as outright theft of the other side's documents].[53] Wandell comments:

---

[49] Ibid., pp. 20–21.
[50] Ibid., p. 28.
[51] Ibid., pp. 24–25.
[52] Ibid., p. 31.
[53] Ibid. pp.36–37.

You should not yield to the temptation to read your adversary's briefs, or examine his private memorandum, which may accidentally fall into your hands, or which you may, unknown to him, find an opportunity of scrutinizing. Such conduct is unfair, beneath the dignity of a respectable lawyer.[54]

Conclusion

"You Should Not" is more than a period piece. It is a document which reflects both the origins of many of our modern ideas about legal ethics and professional responsibility as well as the changing notions of proper behavior that surfaced in the last quarter of the nineteenth century. It is a book that witnesses the insecurity felt by the elite members of a changing legal profession, changing demographically, culturally, ethnically, and economically. Above all, it is a document which shows how the American legal profession's quest for dignity and respectability continued to be a major theme of juristic writing throughout the nineteenth century.[55]

---

[54] Ibid., pp.36–37.
[55] See, M. Bloomfield, *American Lawyers in a Changing Society* (Cambridge, Mass., 1976).

"YOU SHOULD NOT."

A BOOK FOR LAWYERS, OLD AND YOUNG,

CONTAINING

THE ELEMENTS OF LEGAL ETHICS.

By SAMUEL H. WANDELL,

COUNSELLOR AT LAW, OF THE NEW YORK BAR,

Author of "The Law of Inns, Hotels and Boarding Houses," "The Law
Relating to Disposition of Decedents' Real Estate,"
"The Law of the Theatre," etc.

" I charge you by the law,
Whereof you are a well-deserving pillar."
—Merchant of Venice, Act IV, Scene 1.

———

ALBANY, N. Y.:
MATTHEW BENDER, LAW PUBLISHER.
1896.

PLATED AND PRINTED BY
WILLIAM BOYD, ALBANY, N. Y.

PREFACE.

NOTHING need be said by way of apology for this little book which is intended as a code of "danger signals" for the members of the legal profession, who, in the busy race for success at the Bar, have too little time for the study of ethics.

If, however, reason were asked for its publication, I would respectfully quote a passage from the comprehensive "Essay on Professional Ethics," by Hon. George Sharswood, wherein he says:

"There is, perhaps, no profession, after that of the sacred ministry, in which a high-toned morality is more imperatively necessary than that of the law. There is certainly, without exception, no profession in which so many temptations beset the path to swerve from the line of strict integrity; in which so many delicate and difficult questions of duty are continually arising. There are pitfalls and mantraps at every step, and the mere youth, at the very outset of his career, needs often the prudence and self-denial, as well as the moral courage, which commonly belong to riper years. High moral principle is his only safe guide; the only torch to light his way amidst darkness and obstruction.''

This volume has been penned at odd moments; it has been written ''with malice toward none, with charity toward all.'' It is submitted with the hope that its contents will be found interesting and profitable to lawyers of all ages, as indicated by its title.

WORLD BUILDING, New York City, November 1, 1895.

SAMUEL H. WANDELL.

CONTENTS.

———

———

APPENDIX.

YOU SHOULD NOT.

I.—YOURSELF IN GENERAL.

You should not be careless or negligent about your personal appearance. A soiled shirt bosom, dirty collar and greasy or frayed garments bespeak a mind that has grown rusty, and habits which need reforming. Dress neatly, and keep yourself looking respectable. You can do this without being a dude. The seedy looking attorney can usually be counted upon to turn out to be a "briefless barrister."

You should not be afraid to change your location or your professional relations if thereby it seems reasonably certain that you will be substantially benefitted. A change of office, residence or partnership should not be made hastily, but if it seems reasonably sure that such a change will be to your advantage, you should not hesitate because some one calls your attention to the old proverb that "a rolling stone gathers no moss." This is not an age of moss-backs, and you must push yourself to the front or you will never get there.

You should not imagine that you can succeed at the bar unless you work hard in the profession. Great lawyers are made by hard work and diligent application. If you have not the willingness to devote all your time and energies to your client's cause, if you are not willing to be a slave to your profession, you had better surrender your diploma and seek some more congenial occupation. The law is not the proper field for a lazy man.

You should not get the mistaken idea that it pays a lawyer to become noted as sharp and tricky. Judges and juries despise tricksters and soon take their measure. Do not resort to low cunning, but fight your battles manfully. You can be artful, but never be dishonorable.

You should not neglect your business engagements. If you make an appointment to meet a man at the office or at some other place, be there on time. If you promise to prepare some papers by a day certain, see that they are ready by that time, even if you have to burn a little midnight oil once in a while in order to accomplish it. In this way you will achieve a reputation for punctuality and promptness.

You should not practice law with the idea that your profession is only designed as a means of money getting; you should not devote your whole life to the abject service of Mammon. There are lawyers who, it seems, erect a golden calf in the office as soon as they are admitted to the bar, and who spend their best energies and talents in its worship. Yours is a calling of dignity and honor, and you should honor your vocation. You might as well hang out the three balls which denote the calling of the pawn-broker, as to develop into a scheming, flinty-hearted lawyer, whose sole desire is personal aggrandizement and wealth.

You should not be conceited and imagine that the whole world is prostrate at your feet in admiration of your transcendent abilities. It will make you universally disliked and will cause people to speak slightingly of you. The study of the law should have a tendency to make you very humble as you obtain glimpses of the vast fields of knowledge which may be traversed, and as you ascertain what deep caverns and what hidden springs of learning exist which you may explore. Whenever you think of yourself as one of the brightest lights of the legal firmament, as the most resplendent star in the whole galaxy of your competitors, pause and read the wise opinions of Lord Eldon, the commentaries of Kent and Blackstone, the Equity Jurisprudence of Story, the Constitutional Law of Pomeroy, the Institutes of Bouvier; you will then see how much there is of the science which no one, however gifted, can, in one short lifetime, thoroughly master. He can, at best, obtain but a superficial knowledge of the whole system of our jurisprudence; he can but admire its beauty, symmetry and entirety; he can never master its details and intricacies.

You should not fail to acquire the habit of steady application. It is an important factor in your success in life. It will enable you to accomplish much more than your rival who works spasmodically. In your years of study for the bar, practice this virtue; after your entrance upon this sphere of your life-work, apply it. Pluck and perserverance conquer all obstacles and win the battle with fate. They shape and mould your destiny.

You should not fail to be energetic. Energy is like the locomotive ; without its aid the train can not move. In this country the plodders are out of place; they are distanced by the man of energy and push. The energetic men settle and clear the wilderness, build the cities, establish the manufactories, weave the mighty web of commerce that unites nations and encircles the entire globe. You may possess talent, but you must have energy in order to succeed. If you are not inclined to push yourself forward, you will always see some one stepping into the place you desire, just before you get to it.

You should not be imprudent, but you should combine caution, discretion and good judgment with energy. Activity, misdirected, is but little better than idleness. If you are cautious and prudent you can cultivate your judg-

ment to a great degree of accuracy. "Look
before you leap "is an excellent motto. Do not
act hastily, without consideration.

You should not lack perserverance in your
undertakings. Do not get discouraged and fail
to continue to the end. The success of Napo-
lean and Cæsar was due to their fixedness of
purpose and the firmness of their resolutions.
Nil desperandum should be a phrase to conjure
with your daily walks in life. There can be no
assured success without perseverance.

You should not forget the oath taken by
you upon admission to the bar. It was not a
meaningless form of words, but a sacred obligation which should be binding throughout
your entire professional career. By it you
pledged yourself to be honest and honorable
with the court, upright with your client, fair and
courteous to your professional brethren, and
just toward the public at large. These pledges
were involved in the spirit, if not in the letter,
of the obligation then assumed by you ; you
were, by admission to practice law, constituted
an officer of the court, and assumed certain
responsibilities, which should not be evaded.

II.—YOUR OFFICE.

You should not suffer your office to become disorderly, nor should you let the dust of ages accumulate on books, shelves, desks and chairs, or in unused corners. Some lawyers keep their offices looking more like a dingy den or a forgotten crypt than like a place of business. The enterprising attorney who keeps up with the times will always have his office looking neat and orderly. Fossils are generally found imbedded in dirt.

You should not permit your office to become the headquarters of a lounger's club, under the impression that you are thereby gaining in popularity. The people who have nothing to do but to talk and smoke about the office during business hours will never line your pockets with greenbacks. Don't keep open house for idlers or gossips in a law office. They might as well steal your library or your pocket-book as to rob you of your time, which is your only working capital.

You should not keep your office blue with

tobacco smoke ; you should not smoke continually during business hours at the office.
It will interfere with your work and prevent
you from concentrating your mind upon it.
Then, too, excessive smoking is apt to make
you dreamy, lethargic and lazy ; besides that,
you must remember that to many ladies and
to some men, tobacco smoke is extremely
offensive. You should be careful about knock-
ing ashes on the floor, or on desks or chairs,
and should avoid the pernicious habit of leaving the fragrant "stubs" of half smoked
Havannas about the office promiscuously.

You should not locate your office in some
unfrequented street, or in some unknown or
unsuitable building. Above all things, do not
locate in a block which has a disreputable
name. Do not be too anxious to secure a cheap
office. You may save a little on your rent by
such methods, but you will probably loose a
great deal out of your income. Always try to
establish yourself in the business centre of the
place in which you are practicing ; it brings
you into prominence, and it will, in the end,
secure you valuable clients. You should

select, in a city, a good commercial block, which is well known in trade circles, and where business men are accustomed to go to do business; a block in which a bank is located is always desirable for a lawyer. Then, too, get into a building which is well filled with business offices. The tenants of a block in a city are a small community in themselves. Do not be afraid to get into a building where there are other lawyers; it is much better to be in a place where people are in the habit of going to obtain legal advice and assistance, than to be where you are the only lawyer on the premises. You may be, in the latter case, the monarch of all you survey, but your kingdom will often be a barren and unfruitful realm.

III.—YOUR BUSINESS.

You should not brag about your business or tell people what a smart person you are. You should not on every possible occasion boast of how successful you have been at the bar. If you have ability, people will find it out, and they are always apt to distrust a "blow-hard." Silence is golden when praising yourself to others.

You should not tell all you know about your cases or be anxious to let the public know what a wonderful array of facts you have with which to sustain your client's cause; if you do, your adversary may ascertain your strong points and be prepared for them. Keep your business matters to yourself and do not let professional secrets escape you unwittingly. Therefore, don't talk about your clients' affairs, for no one cares to employ a "gabbling solicitor."

You should not conduct you law business without any method or system. Have a place for everything and everything in its place.

Have a time for everything and do everything on time. If you are apt to forget important matters during the hurry and bustle of the day, make it a rule to prepare a list of your duties and appointments beforehand, and consult it from time to time.

You should not waste the precious hours of business in lounging, idle gossip, newspaper and novel reading. You will by such habits entirely loose sight of what you might accomplish during the day. There is always something for a lawyer to do if he has the inclination to work and can remember what is to be done. You should concentrate your mind upon your business early in the day and let your faculties remain intent upon your duties and engagements. Learn to be frugal and conscientious with your time and do not fool it away.

You should not be extravagant and run heavily in debt, or spend your money like a prince. There is no profession in which the income is so uncertain and variable as that of law. The receipts of the business are fluctuating, and the income of one year can not be taken as a criterion for estimating what that of the next

year will be. Of course well-established practitioners and corporation lawyers have a more tan-
gible annuity than those who are struggling up
the hill or are dependent upon the varying for-
tunes of legal conflicts for a competency. The
old time adage, "always a feast or a famine,"
applies to lawyers the world over. When
money comes into a lawyer's hands it is usually
in large amounts, and it often gives the pleased
possessor the slip before he is aware. Some
lawyers never find the dish of gold at the bot-
tom of the rainbow which they pursue through
life. You should, therefore, be careful to keep
a reserve fund laid by, and to steer clear from
financial embarrassments of all kinds. You
can spend money judiciously, and yet escape
the imputation of being niggard. Lawyers
usually work hard, live well and die poor,
although there are exceptions to the rule.

You should not engage in any outside business and try to speculate. If you wish to rise
high in your profession, and to succeed at the
bar, you can not run a manufactory, smelt
ore, embark in mercantile adventures, trade
horses, sell patent rights and real estate, deal

on change, devote your time and talents in a dozen different channels, and at the same time become a good lawyer. The gun which scatters the shot, seldom hits the mark. Remember that "the law is a jealous mistress," and she will jilt you, if you are found coquetting with another. You must be true, earnest and constant, if you would retain her favor.

You should not connect or identify yourself in business with an unlucky man. The chances are ten to one that he alone is to blame for his misfortunes, and that you will suffer by his faults.

You should not endorse checks, drafts or notes for the accommodation of your friends or business acquaintances. You should not incur any liability for mere friendship's sake, which you may be called upon to pay. Make it a universal rule never to endorse for any one, and stick to it. It is better to endure your friend's frown and displeasure than to settle for his debts some day, as you might be obliged to do.

You should not pester your friends and

acquaintances with continual applications for
loans of money. There is no bore so much to
be dreaded as the one who is always asking
for a money accommodation, and whose memory is so treacherous that he forgets all about
it after he gets the money. It is a bad plan to
constantly loan money to your friends. It
may cause hard feelings if you insist on your
rightful dues, and you may lose considerable
cash by being too free to respond to the
demands of your friends. The advice of
Polonious to the departing Laertes is to be
commended:

> " Neither a borrower nor a lender be ;
>   For a loan oft loses both itself and friend,
>   And borrowing dulls the edge of husbandry."

You should not neglect to study human
nature and to read character by physiognomy.
This knowledge is acquired by observation, experience and comparison, although to some
people it seems to come intuitively. This
quality of knowledge is invaluable to a lawyer
in selecting a jury.

You should not neglect any opportunity
for obtaining general information. It is in-

valuable to a lawyer. He can never know too much about anything. A thorough knowledge of the physiology of man, the anatomy of the horse, the secrets of theraputics and chemistry, the proper methods of agriculture, the construction of machinery, the operation of railroads, the latest discoveries in science and the mechanical arts, the customs and regulations of trade, and also a thousand and one other things which might be mentioned are all useful to a lawyer in his practice. He has to cross-examine physicians, engineers, surveyors, railroad men, experts in mechanical inventions, farmers, merchants, book-keepers, real estate agents, bankers, insanity experts and many others. He never knows what evidence will be brought up by his opponent on the trial of an action. He should be as well prepared as possible on all subjects, and to that end should always keep his eyes and ears open to gain knowledge ; no class of information should be despised. Observation is a great teacher in such matters.

You should not procrastinate in your business matters. Learn to be prompt and vigil-

ant in transacting all legal matters, and clients
will soon seek you, and give you business.
The lawyer who never tries his cases unless he
is forced into it by his opponent, or scolded
into it by his own client, who is forever putting
off his work until the last day in the afternoon,
is not the one whom people will employ to enforce a doubtful claim, or to vigorously prosecute a difficult case.

IV.— YOUR CLIENTS.

You should not deal with a client as you would with an outside party. You should be cautious about taking a mortgage or other security from him, for the law is extremely suspicious of any and all transactions between attorney and client, and regards all dealings whereby the attorney obtains an advantage over the client as presumptively fraudulent; the law throws upon the attorney the burden of proof in order to show that the same was honest and straightforward. In case the client ever questions the fairness of his lawyer's conduct, the latter has the laboring oar. It is never safe to deal with a client whereby you acquire some pecuniary benefit, unless you have an unimpeachable witness present, so that you can show there was no trickery or undue advantage practiced.

You should not purchase anything from your clients which is in litigation, and concerning which you are acting as the attorney. The attorney, in order to support such a purchase, must show that he paid as much as could be obtained from any other person. The same rule prevails as regards a sale by the attorney to the client. Where beneficial contracts or conveyances have been obtained by the attorney from the client during the relationship, and which were connected with the subject of pending litigation, the courts have usually allowed them to stand as security for what was actually due the attorney, and have declared the purchases to be merely trusts.

You should not endeavor to stir up quarrels or to provoke litigation; especially as between husbands and their wives, or between members of the same family. The beautitude, "Blessed are the peace-makers," includes lawyers within its scope and meaning. Your clients will often seek you, inflamed with rage and excitement, anxious for revenge. It is the lawyer's duty to keep them out of unnecessary and vindictive law-suits. Then, too, you should remember that there is often more money for an attorney in settling cases out of court than in trying them. Be cautious about beginning litigations, or carrying on cases which only enrich you, and beggar all the rest.

You should not advise a client to commence an action where the chances of defeat are almost certain, so that you can get a fee out of the case. You should give honest advice, and not play upon the ignorance of those who seek your assistance. It is your duty to plainly inform a client of the whole truth about his case; if his grounds of action are insufficient, if the evidence is wanting to sustain it, if the outlook is extremely doubtful, tell your client so at once, and prevent him from embarking in a dangerous and disastrous litigation. You are paid to give your opinion to him on account of your superior learning and experience; you should give it candidly and honestly. If you coax a man into commencing a law-suit, in which he is defeated, he will usually throw the entire blame upon your shoulders. Therefore, you should not urge a client into a litigation. There are, of course, many contingencies and uncertainties which you cannot foresee, being only a mortal, in considering the advisability of beginning an action, but if the case looks shady and doubtful, if your possible victory will be but a hairs-breadth escape from almost certain defeat, you had better avoid the matter entirely. Defeats in court are bad advertisements for a lawyer.

You should not take up every case that is offered you. Learn to discriminate in the selection of cases. Do not espouse the cause of every man or woman who wishes to employ you. Try to select clients who are worthy of legal assistance, who have right and justice on their side, and do not engage in a case where the entire prosecution or defence will neces-sarily consist of a tissue of falsehoods, inter-woven by legal skill. You may get into trouble sometimes with unconsciable clients and disreputable cases. At best they will in-jure your standing at the bar.

You should not enter into collusion with a husband and a wife to secure a divorce, or be a party to a put-up job to obtain a bill of divorce for the mutual accommodation of both parties; neither should you have anything to do with a case of this character which is not perfectly straightforward and honorable. Be-ware how you juggle with the machinery of the

courts in divorce matters. Hesitate to pander
to the base designs of some would-be client,
who, having no legal grounds of action, desires
to circumvent the law, and defeat its provisions
by artifice and fraud ; do not let him make
you the cat's-paw to pull out his coveted chest-
nuts from the blaze, for you may get singed in
the operation. Shun all shyster tricks and
nefarious practices of that kind, and do not
barter your honor and reputation for a glitter-
ing fee. Do not have very many divorce cases,
anyhow, and be square and honest in what few
you are engaged in.

You should not collect money for your
clients and retain it in your own hands, or
mingle it with your private funds. You may
be perfectly honest in so doing, and intend to
pay it over ; but, nevertheless, in a moment of
weakness, you may yield to the temptation to
use it temporarily to relieve some real or fan-
cied desire or necessity. Don't do this under
any circumstances, for it is like driving a nail
into your professional coffin. It may not be
convenient to replace the sum when your client
calls and asks you for a settlement, in which

case you might be tempted to conceal from him
the fact that you had received it, and to resort
to subterfuges in order to put him off. If you
do this you are paving the way to a reputation
for rascality and meanness which you do not
deserve, perhaps, and which will result in the
client transferring his affections to another
and more reliable attorney.

You should not betray a confidence that is
reposed in you as a lawyer. If a person states
a case to you, and if for any reason you are not
employed by him, or should you yourself
decide not to accept a retainer from him, you
have no right to make known to the adversary
or to any one the communications which were
made to you. The law office should be as invio-
late as the confessional. Neither have you
the right to engage in a case against one who
has offered to employ you and who has con-
sulted you. After a man has unbosomed himself to you in the sacred confidence that exists
between the attorney and the client, it is little
better than knavery to turn on him, and use
the information so obtained to defeat his cause.
Attorneys should so conduct themselves that

any one in need of advice or assistance may state their matters freely, without reserve, and know that the confidence will be respected.

V.—YOUR FEES.

You should not omit to exact a good retaining fee in advance before commencing an action or engaging in a defense. A client pays more willingly and freely at the outset, when he is fresh for the fray and eager for battle, than when he is disheartened by delay or discouraged by defeat.

You should not undervalue your professional services and get into the habit of charging low prices, thereby hoping to secure business. Don't try to achieve a reputation as a *cheap* lawyer. People usually estimate the value of anything by its price, and cheap services are not appreciated. You should not overcharge your client, and so drive him away, but you should ask a good, fair compensation for what you do, without being extortionate.

You should not get into the habit of giving free advice, thinking that thereby you will secure the favor of those who consult you professionally. Your grocer will always expect you to pay for the goods which you take away from his store, and why should he not pay for the knowledge which he takes away from your office ? By usually charging a moderate counsel fee, you will add considerably to your annual income, and the general public will consider your opinion worth something if they have to pay for it. You will, in the long run, gain clients and elevate yourself in the estimation of the people who consult you by refusing to allow them to enjoy a "free lunch" of legal advice at your office.

You should not sue clients for the recovery of fees, unless the amount involved is large and you stand a good chance of obtaining your money. It is far better to *never* bring such suits, which are looked upon with suspicion and will prejudice the public mind, no matter what the merits of the controversy may be. An eminent writer truly says that it is better for the attorney to be a loser than to have a public contest with his client. In France such a suit, while maintainable, is yet considered dishonorable, and should an advocate attempt to enforce his rights in this manner, he would be

stricken from the rolls. In England a counsellor or barrister cannot maintain a suit for
fees, while the less distinguished attorneys,
who are not allowed to speak in court, are permitted to recover by action for services.

You should not take up a long, tedious
litigation without having some agreement beforehand with your client as to what your compensation is to be. Generally speaking, it is
far better to have a prior understanding as to
the price of services to be rendered in all cases,
and in important matters, the agreement should
be in writing. In the event of the attorney
being obliged to enforce his rights by suit,
the contract determines the troublesome question of the value of the services, while in its
absence, testimony of other lawyers must be
resorted to in order to establish it. Juries are
apt to regard unfavorably any testimony of
this character, and to apply the adage, "hawks
will never pick hawks' eyes out," to attorneys
who are testifying to the value of services in
favor of a professional brother. The writer to
whom we previously referred observes: "No
one can ever have seen such a cause tried

without feeling that the Bar had received by it an impulse downward in the eyes of bystanders and the community. The case is thrown into the jury-box, to be decided at haphazard, according as the twelve men may chance to think or feel."

You should not "fleece" your clients. Do not imagine that a license to practice law carries with it the right to become a pirate on the high seas of life, so that you can plunder every one who comes within your power. Some lawyers have grown rich by such means, but no amount of money can secure them the confidence of the public. We knew an instance of an attorney to whom a promissory note was entrusted for collection by a business man. The amount of the note was one hundred dollars. The lawyer simply wrote a dunning letter to the maker of the note, who immediately called and paid it. The lawyer pocketed the entire amount, charging the client that sum for counsel fee and services in the matter. Such outrageous conduct should result in the disbarment of an attorney who would so degrade the profession. You ought always to charge a good, fair fee for your services, but, at the same time, you should be reasonable, and not commit legalized larceny. You should endeavor to deal with your clients so that they will seek you in the future when they are in need of legal assistance. That is the only way to build up a large practice, and to insure a successful business career.

VI.—YOURSELF IN COURT.

You should not pull your moustache, run your fingers through your hair, pick your nose or teeth, nor adjust your collar and necktie when addressing the court or a jury. Neither should you rub your hands together as though you were washing them in invisible water. Such motions betray nervousness, and a lack of self-confidence. Your toilet should be made in the ante-room. When in court you should not by any means betray your want of confidence in yourself or your client's cause. A calm, self-possession, free from conceit, is always pleasing in court.

You should not lose your temper in court. It puts you at a disadvantage immediately. Do not be thrown off your guard in this way. Self-control is like a coat-of-mail to a lawyer; without it, he has no protection from his adversary's shafts, and is always at the mercy of some sarcastic archer.

You should not resort to blackguard and

buffoonery in trying a case. Such tricks of
the trade are the ear marks of the pettifogger.
A well-directed shot, a sally of wit, a quick
repartee are not to be prohibited by this rule;
but the "bluffer," who tries his case in such
a manner that it is plain to be seen he depends
more on his tongue than his evidence to win,
who conducts himself as though he were in a
bar-room rather than in a court-house, is
within its meaning. There are such lawyers
in almost every community. Younger lawyers
should not take them as models, for they are
not worthy of imitation.

You should not go into court unless your
case is ready for trial; you should master the
technical legal propositions involved in it, and
have a good theory to sustain your contention,
which you can support by facts. Understand
the principles of law involved in the issue, and
prepare your brief by selecting authoritative
cases. You should know just what evidence
you can produce upon the trial; therefore
remember that

You should not put too much faith in what
your client tells you about his cause. He is an

interested party, and will be apt to state facts as favorable to his side of the controversy as possible. Do not fail to see the witnesses yourself, whenever it is possible, and to ascertain from them personally what they will testify to, before going into court. Never neglect to prepare your facts thoroughly before trial, as well as to investigate the legal questions involved.

You should not attempt to deceive the court, or to mislead the judge. If the presiding judge once detects you in any such attempt to impose upon him, he will never feel disposed to grant you a favor, and he will always look with suspicion upon your arguments. If you have the confidence of the court, you have half won your point, provided it is well taken, and in matters of discretion, you will be well treated. Beware how you abuse the confidence of a judicial officer.

You should not be too sure of winning your case. Never be entirely sanguine of success, or it may put you off your guard, and you may overlook some important point in the preparation of the cause for trial. Many a good case has been lost by the over-confidence of the attorney. You ought to prepare each case thoroughly, no matter how easy it seems at first sight.

You should not become a mere "case law-lawyer," always at sea unless you can find a reported decision to sustain your point. Learn thoroughly the fundamental principles of the law, and seek to apply them in your practice. Do not loose sight of principles in searching for precedents. Precedents should yield to principles in all cases; the converse of this proposition is never true.

You should not cross-examine a witness at random, without yourself knowing why you ask your questions. Do not make the cross-examination an opportunity for "showing off" to your client and the court. Be sure you know the witness before you undertake to lead him by the nose. There are probably as many cases injured by an injudicious cross-examination as there are cases benefitted by the assistance of a skillful cross-examiner. The witness on the direct examination seldom has an opportunity to tell his story completely, or to relate all that he knows on the subject beneficial to the party who has summoned him. The attorney who calls the witness is usually so trammelled by the rules of evidence that he can not draw out the whole thread of the narrative; it is pulled out by jerks, in a disjointed manner. It is then that the unwary cross-examiner often commits a grevious error by going over the whole field with the witness and patching up the holes and spaces which his adversary was compelled to leave, and thus drawing out the whole story from the witness. He thereby shows to the jury just what the opposing counsel desired to, but could not, under the rulings of the court. Before you ask a witness a question on the cros-sexamination, just ask yourself, mentally, this question: "What will he answer?" If you are apprehensive that his answer might damage you and aid the adversary, do not ask the question at all. Seldom ask a witness "how" he knows, or "why" he remembers, as his explanation might injure you.

You should not fail to memorize all the facts which you expect to be able to prove by the witnesses, both upon the direct examina-

tion of your witnesses, and upon the cross-
examination of your adversary's witnesses.
Then examine in relation to such facts in the
proper order, thus building up your case from
the foundation.

You should not allow yourself to be dis-
turbed or disconcerted by unfavorable evidence ; it will loose half its power to work you
an injury if you maintain a calm demeanor in
court. Many people form their estimate of
the value of evidence by simply observing its
effect upon the examining attorneys.

You should not neglect to restrain and
repress the pert, forward and "smart" witnesses who will always injure the cause they
wish to aid by self-assurance and offensive
zeal. Toward all such be dignified and never
allow them to become familiar with you.

You should not put irrelevant questions to
a witness ; do not question without an object
in view. Frame your interrogatories carefully
so that you will be able to maintain your
position if your adversary objects, which he is
always apt to do.

You should not object to your opponent's questions without some tenable ground to fortify yourself, when called upon to give the reason for such objections. Do not constantly interpose and then withdraw objections. It will appear foolish in the eyes of the jury, and will afford the court just ground for criticism.

You should not call a witness yourself whom you know will surely be called by your opponent. If your adversary calls the witness, he vouches for his credibility to the court and to the jury, and you have the wide field of cross-examination open before you. Anything which the witness may state favorable to your side of the controversy will cut your opponent like a two-edged sword, as he is deprived of the power of impeaching his own witness.

You should not try to prove too much by an unfriendly witness. Bring him at once to the vital point on which his testimony is essential, and have done with him as soon as possible. Do not give him an opportunity to explain anything, or to modify, or to correct his previous statements. Some witnesses cunningly conceal their antipathy until on the stand they exhibit it clearly. Toward all such the attorney may properly show righteous indignation, and deal with them with great firmness; he should try to bring out and show the reasons for such hostility if possible.

You should not lose your temper with a stupid witness. Do not get out of patience at his blunders, and fly at him. Keep yourself under control at all times, but especially when you are dealing with the blunders of your own witness. Encourage the witness of dull perceptions; frame your questions to meet his understanding; lead him gently from mistaken statements to giving the correct version if possible. It is here that the tact of the advocate is seen to the best advantage.

You should not yield to the temptation to read your adversary's briefs, or examine his private memorandum, which may accidentally fall into your hands, or which you may, unknown to him, find an opportunity of scrutinizing. Such conduct is unfair, ungentlemanly and unprofessional, beneath the dignity of a respectable lawyer. There have been attorneys who were known to sneak into the offices of their opponent to pry into his secrets, thus seeking to ascertain in advance of the trial the theory of the prosecution or defense, as the case might be, and to enable them to prepare for it. An advantage thus gained is a mean one, and a lawyer who would stoop to anything of the kind is a disgrace to the profession. He should be so frowned upon by respectable members of the profession as to become a pariah at the Bar.

VII.—YOUR ASSOCIATIONS.

You should not become noted for being tricky and technical with the bar. Treat your opponents manfully and courteously. Do not take petty advantages, such as defaults, in order to get a small fee for yourself. Be generous to your brother advocates, and let your word be as good as your written stipulation or your bond.

You should not get into the habit of speaking disrespectfully of your brother lawyers. You will gain nothing yourself by continually harping on the weakness of your competitors, or by trying to belittle them in the community. There may be a "beam" in your eye which obscures your vision so that you do not see your own faults which are plainly visible to others. Again, you should remember that if you talk about others, they will learn of it, and will be apt to say something about you, which will not be flattering. No one ever yet built up a good character upon the ruins of his neighbor's reputation. If you cannot conscientiously speak well of some attorney within the circle of your acquaintance, do not say anything at all about him unless it is necessary to do so ; in which case be guarded in your utterances.

You should not forget to make friends whose influence and business relations will be of assistance to you in securing a clientage. When a young lawyer starts in the profession, his first business generally comes from his friends.   There are abler and better lawyers who are his competitors ; he is not at first employed because of his experience and superior ability, but because some one who knows him, desires to help him, from purely motives of personal regard.   Therefore, in your earlier years cultivate the friendship of desirable people and it will be the stepping-stone to securing their patronage.   At the same time be cautious, lest you should be taken for a fawning sycophant.

You should not be hasty in forming partnership relations with your brethren of the Bar. A partnership is akin to a marriage in point of importance and solemnity, and should be duly

considered in all its phases. A partnership in
which the several members are each workers,
and each bring their due proportion of business to the firm, is desirable on account of thereby securing an equitable division of labor, provided, of course, that each member is honest
and reliable. You had better hang a mill-stone
about your neck and then attempt to swim
through the ocean, than to tie yourself up in
partnership with a drone, a knave, a sluggard,
or a man of blemished character or of doubtful
reputation.

You should not have too many confidential
and intimate friends. You should not let the
latch-strings of your heart hang out to every
one, nor should you be hasty in giving your
confidence to the persons with whom you asso-
ciate. Be cautious about making friends, and
be sure that they are worthy of your friendship
before you bestow it upon them. You should
be polite and courteous to all whom you meet,
but you should be wary about exchanging
acquaintanceship for friendship. You should
be true to the friends you have, but you should
not have too many.

"The friends thou hast, and their adoption tried,
    Grapple them to thy soul with hooks of steel ;
But do not dull thy palm with entertainment
    Of each new-hatched, unfledged comrade."

VIII.—YOUR MORALS.

You should not be careless of your morals. Good personal habits are as essential as are good business habits to your success in life. Good habits are a pass-port of good character, and an assurance of personal integrity and worth.

You should not cultivate bad habits. They are the only handicaps in the great race for success. They foster boorishness and selfishness, and tend toward the undermining of manners and of morals. Habits are the corner-stones of character; if the foundation be carelessly laid, in material which is subject to disintegration, the whole structure is apt to crumble and fall. Humanity is writhing in the fetters and chains forged by bad habits. Habit is an exacting task-master, who requires constant service, and who pays but poorly for it. A lawyer should be careful of his habits.

You should not stifle your conscience, nor sear it as with a hot iron. If it tells you that a contemplated action is wrong, if it revolts at your conduct, forbear to continue in what this silent monitor reminds you is not right. Think of a mariner navigating the trackless ocean, who would refuse to consult his chart and compass, or even to look at the stars, least he might thereby become warned of the vicinity of sunken rocks or the proximity of breakers. And yet, he would be no more a fool than the lawyer who is ever deaf to the promptings of the "still, small voice," which enables him to distinguish between the right and the wrong,

You should not forget that "honesty is the best policy" for a lawyer. The lawyer is the servant of the public. He is dependent for his business and support upon the good opinion of his fellowmen. If he is noted as being shrewd and unprincipled, he will depend upon rogues and sharpers principally for his business, and they often succeed in beating an attorney out of his pay. If a lawyer is known as an upright, conscientious and honorable man, of good principles, of unimpeachable intergrity, he will be patronized by the better class of people. He will have the business of large estates, wealthy

persons and rich corporations ; he will frequent-
ly be selected as referee in important cases.
It *pays* an attorney to be strictly honest and
upright in all his dealings. Such a lawyer will
succeed far better in the long run than his more
brilliant but less conscientious rival.

You should not suborn witnesses nor falsify
evidence ; you ought to endeavor to elevate,
instead of to degrade the morals of the community in which you live. You should not try
to defeat the course of justice, or to block its
wheels by unfair, unprofessional methods. Be
honorable and fair to your opponent, to the
bar, to the court and to the jury.
    "This above all, to thine own self be true."

You should not use the legal profession as
a shield and a screen to protect you in levying
blackmail. Never engage in dirty jobs, or in
shady transactions, which are hatched up for
the purpose of extorting money from some one
who is not legally obliged to pay it, but who
might do so as a matter of expediency, rather
than suffer publicity and annoyance. As a
matter of policy, as well as of principle, you
cannot afford to do this.

You should not send a dunning epistle which is written upon a postal card. It is an offence under the United States laws.

You should not send threatening letters through the mail; that is also an offense. You should be careful and guarded in what you threaten to do on paper.

You should not write to a person from whom you are trying to collect a bill, stating that unless he settles you will institute criminal proceedings, get him arrested or expose some secret which is in your possession, and which he is anxious to keep from the public. If you do so, you may be offending against the law forbidding blackmail and extortion. You may get into serious complications by sending such a letter. Such a course of collecting is not decent or reputable.

You should not ante-date the jurat of an affidavit which is sworn to before you as a notary, commissioner or other officer. You should not use such an office as a shield or cover for fraud or connivance. The courts have disbarred attorneys for just such dishonest practices.

You should not under any circumstances forfeit the respect and confidence of a judge. If the court esteems an attorney and believes him to be strictly honorable, many instances will arise in which such lawyer will be favored ; many cases are brought into court the decision of which is wholly a matter of discretion. The court will never decide such cases in favor of a dishonest, discourteous, and disreputable attorney, but will prefer to favor the man of clean record, and unimpeachable character.

You should not pack a jury, nor endeavor to secure a verdict by corrupt, unfair and dishonorable means. Never be guilty of bribery, directly or indirectly. If juries are corrupt, it is because lawyers or suitors use measures to debase and improperly influence them. The morals of the Bar influence the morals of the jury. If you can not win honorably, then suffer defeat, rather than smirch yourself with disreputable practices.

VIII.— YOUR HEALTH.

You should not fail to preserve your health. A dyspeptic, nervous and sickly man will have up-hill work in the practice of such an exacting profession as the law. Therefore, early in life, remember Shakespeare's advice to

"Have mind upon your health."

You should not forget that the sedentary habits of a professional man are not conducive to good digestion and perfect health. You should counteract the bad effects of close confinement at the office by living properly, and taking plenty of exercise.

You should not imagine that you are practicising economy by not allowing yourself any vacation, or relaxation from the cares of business, and by keeping yourself constantly at work, without intermission, the entire year; you will, in the end, pay dearly for such folly.

You should not forget that an earnest, dilligent student is prone to undermine and ruin his health. He is apt to be buoyed

up by the delusive hope that he can always
work without cessation. This is a mistake fre-
quently made by the members of the legal
profession.

You should not think that because you can
not see the end of your strength, that it has no
end. No one is possessed of unlimited powers
of endurance. Most cases of physical exhaus-
tion and nervous prostration are due to the fact
that the strength has been overtaxed, and no
opportunity given for recuperation.

You should not forget that good health is
necessary in order to make you a successful
lawyer. Endurance, cheerfulness and vivacity
lend a splendor to eloquence, and add to the
weight of argument or oration. The digestion
often deserves as much credit as the intellect in
the result of a legal conflict.

You should not forget that the lawyer who
possesses health can endure the fatigue of a long
legal contest much better than his sickly and
broken down competitor. The former comes in
on the home-stretch full of vigor and elasticity,
while the latter is as limp as a dish-rag. The

arguments of the one are forcible, powerful and convincing, while those of the other fail to interest the jury, and are often unheeded and but half heard. Genius can never soar to the loftiest peaks, unaided by her consort, good health.

You should not be a spendthrift with your health. It is a lawyer's capital, and should not be impaired; it should be jealously guarded. He can perform twice the amount of labor, to better advantage, and with greater ease, if, early in life, he pays attention to the laws of health, and continues to observe them. If he fails to do this, he will probably break down physically, and will do all his work upon credit, instead of upon capital; the doctors will be his bankers, and he will be obliged to negotiate frequent loans in order to carry on business. This is a ruinous practice as regards health, as well as business and money matters.

You should not neglect physical exercise. All out-of-door sports and past-times are bene ficial to a hard working business or professional man. Yachting, canoeing, hunting, fishing, riding, base-ball, tennis, cricket, gymnastics and other recreations are better than medicine for a lawyer. They make him forget the worries and vexations of his professional life, sweep away the cobwebs from his brain, cause the stagnant blood to circulate, the torpid liver to act, the enfeebled pulse to throb with new vigor ; they give zest and relish to the satiated and capricious appetite. The best lawyers flee from the hot and dusty city in Summer months, and by rolling ocean, limpid lakes and babbling brooks, in woodland glades, on mountain peaks, or in the delights of travel, find enjoyment and rest. Good health is equal to at least fifty per cent more brain power to a professional man. It should be preserved if you have it, and it should be obtained if you have it not.

"Were he not in health,
He would embrace the means to come by it."

APPENDIX.

THE

NATURE AND HISTORY

OF

THE LEGAL PROFESSION.

Definition of Terms.

Attorney.

Sir William Blackstone defines an attorney at law to be "a person put in the place, stead or turn of another, to manage his law concern;"[1] Bacon defines thus, "an attorney at law is appointed to prosecute and defend for his client,"[2] while Comyns states that an attorney in court is "an attorney *ad prosequendum* or *defendum.*"[3] Jacobs says that an attorney is "one that is appointed by another man to do anything in his absence,"[4] which defi-

[1, 3] Blackstone's Commentaries, 25.
[2] Bacon's Abridgment, vol. 1. 183, title "Attorney."
[3] Comyns' Digest, vol. 1, 618.
[4] Jacobs' Dictionary, vol. 1.

nition has been very properly criticised, since an attorney may act both in his client's presence and in his absence. An English writer defines an attorney at law as an officer or member of a court of record, and appointed in the place of another, to transact or manage either his law concerns, and the business incidental thereto, or other affairs which require the professional skill, knowledge, or learning usually possessed by a member of the courts of law."[5] Coke says that "an attorney is an ancient English word, and signifieth one that is set in the turn, stead or place of another; and of these some be private and some be public, as attorneys at law, whose warrant from his master is, *pronit locosuo talem attornatum suum*, which setteth in his turn or place such a man to be his attorney."[6] A later writer defines an attorney at law as "an officer of a court of record, legally qualified to prosecute and defend actions in courts of law on the retainer of clients."[7]

[5] Maughham on **Attorneys**, 4.
[6] Co. Lit. 51, *b.*
[7] Merrifield on **Attorneys**, 2.

Solicitor.

A solicitor is described as a person employed
to follow and take care of suits in equity courts,
and is so recognized by the English courts.
The word in itself is more modern than the old
Saxon word "attorney." Formerly all business in the English Court of Chancery was
conducted by the Six Clerks, and their under
clerks. With the increase of chancery busi
ness the under clerks became a distinct class of
practitioners and were recognized by the court
as "sworn clerks" or "clerks in court." The
advance of commercial and business interests
so developed and multiplied the chancery litigations that these "clerks in court" were
unable to attend to the accumulated business,
and hence originated the "solicitors in equity"
who gave their attention to the transaction of
business in the chancery courts. In 1842 a
statute was passed abolishing the offices of the
Six Clerks in the Court of Chancery.[1] The
custom of applying the term "solicitor" to
proceedings *at law* has been strongly con-
demned.

[1] Stat. 5 and 6 Vict. c. 103, § 1.

The term solicitor is first found in English statutes in 3 Jac. 1, chapter 7, and is used to designate attorneys practicing in courts of equity jurisdiction. The term proctor in English law refers to the practitioners in courts of admiralty jurisdiction and the ecclesiastical courts, and attorney is used to designate those practicing in the common law courts.[2]

Barrister.

This term is said to have been used primarily to denote apprentices, being the first degree in law conferred by the inns of court. As early as the time of Edward I, however, it was employed to denote counsel below the station of serjeant-at-law, Coke states that this degree was anciently preferred to that of serjeant. A barrister must have been three years a member of an inn of court before he can be called to the Bar. After a member of an inn of court has kept twelve terms, he may, without being called, obtain permission to practice *under the bar*, as a special pleader in common law courts or an equity draftsman in equity courts, or as a conveyancer. The barristers are divided

[2] Bouvier's Law Dictionary, 206.

into classes; such as have a patent or precedence, as king's counsel, sit within the bar and wear silk gowns; the other class is termed outer or utter barristers. Bouvier classifies barristers as *ouster*, one who pleads ouster or without the bar; *inner*, a serjeant or king's counsel who pleads within the bar; *vacation*, a counsellor newly called to the bar, who is to attend for several long vacations the exercise of the house.

Serjeant.

The head-covering worn by this order of barristers has been said to have given this denomination. The coif is of ancient origin, and is supposed to have been invented for the purpose of concealing the clerical tonsure, and thus disguising the renegade clerks who were desirous of circumventing the canonical prohibition restraining the clergy from practising in the secular courts. Others assert that it dates from an earlier period, when the higher courts were monopolized by the clergy, and that it was invented by persons not in order, to conceal the want of clerical tonsure.

The title of serjeant has always been considered as highly honorable and as conferring great distinction. By the common law no one could be appointed judge of the superior court who had not attained the degree of the coif, which was only conferred on a barrister of one of the inns of court.

The serjeants were formerly limited to fifteen in number, and enjoyed a monopoly of the practice in the Court of Common Pleas. The statute of 9 and 10 Vict., c. 54, extended to all barristers the privileges of serjeant in the Court of Common Pleas.

Ancient English Statutes.

Under the Gothic constitution every suitor was obliged to appear in person, and no attorney was allowed at common law without the king's special warrant,[3] but the suitor was obliged to appear in court himself whether he was plaintiff or defendant. After each personal appearance the court had the power which held plea by writ to admit him by attorney, but a court that held pleas without writ could not

---

[3] Stiernbook de Jur. Goth, 2, 1, c. 6.

admit a party by attorney without the king had granted a writ *de attornato faciendo.*

In the year 1235 a statute was passed providing that every free man who owed suit to the county, tithing, hundred and wapentake, or to the court of his town, might freely make his attorney to do these suits for him.[1]   A later statute provided that if any serjeant counter, or other, were guilty of any manner of deceit in the king's[2] court, or consented to such deceit, or to aguile the court or a party, and be thereby attainted, he should be imprisoned for a year and a day, and from thenceforth could not be heard to plead in court for any man.   The Westminister statute enacted that in writs of assize, attaint and *juris utrum*, the tenant, after appearance, might make his attorney.[3]   The statute of Gloucester provided that defendants in trespass might make an attorney when an appeal did not lie.[4]

A subsequent statute enacted that persons impleaded in certain courts might make a gen-

1 20 Hen. 3 st. Merton, c. 10.
2 3 Edw. 1, Stat. 1 Westm., c. 29.
3 *Idem*, c. 42.
4 6 Edw. 1 St. Gloucester, c. 8.

eral attorney in all pleas, to sue for them in all pleas moved for or against them during the circuit, until the pleas be determined or the attorney be removed by his master,[8] and the right to appear by attorney was thereafter extended to writs of *proemunire*, to tenants in novel disseisin, to persons outlawed and waived by erroneous legal process, to appellants in an appeal of murder, to the petit jury in attaint, to every natural born subject bailable by law in suits or information or penal statutes, etc.

Appearance by attorney was allowed in France for the first time by letters patent by Philip de Bel, in the year 1240.

Attendance at Court Compelled.

Under the ancient English practice all attorneys were obliged to attend court at certain times, and a non-attendance forfeited the right to practice, and subjected the disobedient attorney to expulsion from the roll. The probable reason for requiring the attendance of attorneys at court was to give them practical experience

---

[8] 13 Edw, 1, c. 8. '

in the rules and in the practice of law. It was
provided in 1573 by a rule of Michaelmas term
(15 Elizabeth) that every attorney of the Court
of Common Pleas should attend in court by
the second return of every term, excepting
Michaelmas term, and by the third return of
that term, on penalty ·of forfeiting three shillings and four pence for each such offense,
unless he should have reasonable excuse for
non-attendance. It was also ordered that all
such attorneys as had been absent and that had
not been engaged in any cause in two years,
should be put off the roll. By a rule in Trinity
term (24 Elizabeth) it was ordered that any
attorney who should absent himself two terms
together from attending at court, except on
account of sickness or other urgent cause,
should no longer be an attorney of the court.
In Easter term (12 Jac. 1, 1615) the rule of 15
Elizabeth was re-enacted with a penalty of
forty shillings for the first offence, and for the
second, expulsion from the court, unless a reasonable excuse was shown. By a rule in Hilary
term of the King's Bench, in 1645, attorneys
were ordered to be put off the roll in case they
did not attend court for three weeks during

Easter. In 1653 it was ordered that all officers
and attorneys of the court should appear in
person upon or before the fourteenth day of
Michaelmas term, and upon or before the
seventh day of every other term, upon penalty
of ten shillings for the first offence, twenty
shillings for the second, and expulsion from
the roll for the third. Attorneys were also
required to be admitted of some inn of court or
chancery, and to be in commons one week in
every term, and take chambers there, if convenient, or, if not, to take chambers or dwell-
ings in some convenient places, and leave proper
notice thereof. And a disobedience to this rule
was punished by expulsion from the roll.

Attorneys were often subjected to severe pen-
alties under the early English law for miscon-
duct in office and other offenses. An incident
is recorded of a learned barrister who was
sentenced to loose both his ears in the pillory,
to degradation from the Bar, to pay a fine of
three thousand pounds, and to be imprisoned
for life. Sometime afterward he published a
pamphlet against the hierarchy and was again
sentenced to loose what remained of his ears,
to pay a fine of five thousand pounds, to be

branded on both his cheeks with the letters, S. L., denoting seditious libeller, and to remain in prison for life.[1]

English System of Regulating Admission.

From an early period regulations as to the admission and qualifications of attorneys have existed in England. Many of the rules of court and statutory provisions relating to the subject have been repeated. The statute of 20 Edward I. required the judges to select the most learned and able attorneys and apprentices to do ser- vice in the courts. The statute of 3 James I. provided for the qualifications of attorneys to be in the future admitted and also for the suf- ficiency. and integrity of those attorneys who were already in practice, providing that none should be suffered to solicit any cause in court but such as were known to be of sufficient and honest disposition. The acts of 6 and 7 Victoria and other statutes prescribed the following qualifications for admission as attorney and solicitor: Execution of a contract in writing

---

[1] Dr. J. Hammond Trumbull's "Blue Laws, True and False," p. 13.

with a practicing attorney or solicitor for the term of five years, or of three years if the clerk be a graduate of either of the universities of Oxford, Cambridge, Dublin, London or Durham, or of the Queen's University, Ireland, or if he have been a member of the Bar, a writer to the signet, a solicitor to the Supreme Court in Scotland, or for ten years a bona fide managing clerk to an attorney; payment of the stamp duty on the contract which amounts to £80; registry or enrollment of the contract in six months thereafter; actual service the prescribed period in the proper business of attorney and solicitor, but one year may be served with the London agent, and if the service is for five years, another year may be served with a barrister or special pleader; due notice of the application for admission, which is posted in several public places where legal notices are usually affixed; fitness and capacity ascertained in examination and certified by the examiners; taking the oath, being formally admitted and enrolled; the registrar's certificate of enrollment and the stamped certificates of the annual payment of the duty.

An attorney who is admitted to any of the

superior courts in England may be admitted to any of the courts of the kingdom, and may act as advocate in any inferior court. If an attorney or solicitor shall practice in any court without obtaining a stamped certificate for the current year, he is incapable of maintaining suit to recover his fees or disbursements. No attorney or solicitor is permitted to have more than two clerks at the same time. No attorney or solicitor, who is confined in a prison or jail, may commence or defend any action, suit or other proceeding in law, equity or bankruptcy or maintain any action to recover fees for business done during his confinement. No attorney or solicitor is permitted to commence any action or suit for his fees until after the expiration of one calendar month after delivery of his bill of costs to the party charged, who may, if he be inclined to dispute the bill, make application and have the bill referred to be taxed, and his attorney's proceedings stayed in the meantime. If the attorney or solicitor do not deliver his bill, the English law permits the client to obtain an order directing him to do so, and also to forthwith deliver all papers and documents of his client relating to the business for which the bill is made out, upon the payment of his just dues. The attorney must take out his certificate annually as long as he continues to practice, which he must enter in one of the courts to which he has been admitted to practice. Certificates were first required by the act of 25 George III, c. 80. If the attorney neglects to take out his certificate his admission is null and void according to the statute of 37 George III, c. 90, and he is subject to an action for a penalty at the suit of a common informer. This statute provided for a re-admission of attorneys who had neglected to take out the annual certificate on payment of all sums due, and such further sums as the court directed. The word "neglect" used in the statute means culpable neglect, and does not apply to a person who has discontinued the practice of his profession, who can be re-admitted without payment of the arrears of duty.

In Ireland the regulations are similar to those in England, and the position of attorney and solicitor is substantially the same. In Scotland there are various degrees of the profession. The most privileged body are the Writers to the Signet, who, with the solicitors before the Supreme Courts, conduct all the business of those courts. The former is the more influential class of practitioners, but both are on an equal footing as practicing "law agents," as they are called. These are both admitted by the Court of Sessions, and have exclusive privileges in that court and in other superior courts; they also practice before the inferior courts. The provincial attorneys are denominated as writers and solicitors. In Aberdeen they are known as advocates. These provincial attorneys are admitted by the various sheriffs or county courts within whose jurisdiction they practice.

Counsel Assigned to Defend Prisoners.

Under the English law the fiction existed that the judge was counsel for the accused, and for a long period the criminal was not allowed the full benefit of counsel to defend him. Formerly his counsel could only argue such legal propositions as the criminal himself could suggest. The privilege of counsel to defend prisoners was gradually extended to all crimes, and the right of the defendant in a criminal trial to employ counsel was recognized. The American constitutional law secures this right to every person accused of crime. The old-time fiction still exists that the court will defend the prisoner if he is unable to defend himself, so that the court will assign an attorney, who is one of its own officers, to defend the criminal is he desires that this be done. An attorney who is thus assigned must act for the defense, and cannot refuse so to do,[1] and his refusal so to act subjects him to punishment for a contempt of court. Unless there be some statutory provision allowing compensation to attorneys who are assigned to defend criminals, they must act without remuneration from the county.[2]

Admission to the Bar.

No one can appear in courts of record and prosecute or defend suits for another unless he

---

[1] Vise v. Hamilton Co., 19 Ill. 18.

[2] Cooley's Constitutional Limitations (3rd ed.), 334; People v. Albany Co., 28 How. Pr. (N. Y.), 22; Wayne Co. v. Waller, 90 Pa. St. 961 ; Case v. Shawnee Co., 4 Kansas, 511; Wright v. State, 3 Heisk (Tenn.), 256 ; Gordon v. Dearborn Co., 52 Ind. 332; Rowe v. Yuba Co., 17 Cal. 61; Elam v. Johnson, 48 Ga. 348 ; Weistad v. Winnebago Co., 20 Wis. 418; Regina v. Forguety, 8 Cox Crim. Cas. 161; Kelley v. Andrew Co. 43 Mo. 338 ; Jones v. Cozens, 16 La. An. 428.

has been regularly admitted to practice according to law. An act authorizing any person of good moral character to act in such capacity, although not admitted, when specially authorized is unconstitutional.[3]   A person not admitted as an attorney cannot be allowed to practice as such under the name of agent.[4]   A person not admitted cannot be substituted in place of the attorney of record by consent.[5]   There is no necessity for admission to the Bar in order to enable a person to practice in justice court, as no attorneys as such are known in that court.[6]

A student at law must serve a clerkship under the personal direction of the attorney with whom his studies are pursued.[7]   The students' certificate should state that such clerkship was served "in the office" of the attorney, and a statement that the clerk had regularly pursued

3 McKoon v. Devries, 3 Barb. 196, Ex parte Brewer, 3 How. Pr. 169 ; Bullard v. Van Tassell, 3 How. Pr. 402.

4 Weir v. Slocum, 8 How. Pr. 397 ; S. C., 1 Code R. 105 ; Budlong v. Van Tassell, 3 How. Pr. 402.

5 Roy v. Hailey, 1 Duer, 637.

6 Bailey v. Delaplain, 1 Sand, 11 ; Hughes v. Mulvey, Idem. 92.

7 Anon. 4 Johns. 191.

the study of the law, under his direction and superintendence, is insufficient in New York State.[8]

The legislature has power to declare that the diploma of a law school should be conclusive evidence of the learning and ability of its possessor.[9]   Citizens of one State are not entitled as matter of right to be admitted to the Bar of another State.[10]

If the admission to the Bar was obtained by fraud, the court will not suffer itself to be imposed upon, but will, under proper knowledge of the facts, strike the offending party from the rolls, and this seems to have been the rule in England.   A case is reported where an attorney and clerk entered into collusion and joined in an affidavit of the execution, of the articles, and the clerk swore to the execution of them and was admitted, and it afterwards appeared that such affidavits were false ; the court ordered the clerk to be struck from the

---

[8] Anon. 3 Johns. 261.

[9] *Ex parte* Cooper, 22 N. Y., 67.

[10] *Ex parte* Henry, 40 N. Y. 560 ; Bradwell *v.* State, 16 Wall (U. S.) 130.

roll and granted an attachment against the attorney for the collusion.[1]

If a student at law is unsuccessful in passing the bar examination, it seems that he has the right to appeal from the order of the Supreme Court denying his admission, as the court acts judicially in the admission of attorneys.[2] The admission is not a ministerial act, and is not therefore the subject of a *mandamus*.[3]

Knowledge and Skill.

In an old work on practice published in England under the title of "The Competent Solicitor," the following essential qualifications of a solicitor are enumerated: "A solicitor ought to have a good natural wit, which wit must be refined by learning; then his learning should be balanced with discretion, and, to manifest all, it is requisite he should have a free and voluble tongue." A subsequent writer adds that the solicitor should be well read in law,

---

1 *Ex parte* Hill 2 W. Bl. 991.
2 *Ex parte* Cooper, 22 N. Y. 67.
3 *In re* Breckenridge, 1 S. R. (Pa.) 187.

vigilant and wary in business, and unwearied in application.

An attorney is liable only for want of ordinary skill and care and the want of reasonable dilligence.[1] He is not answerable for every error or mistake; he ought not to be liable in cases of reasonable doubt.[2] The cases seem to establish that he is liable for the consequences of ignorance or non-observance of the rules of the court, for want of care in preparation of the cases for trial, or of attendance thereon; for mismanagement of the case. He is not liable for errors in judgment on points of uncertain or doubtful construction.[3] It is held that want of ordinary care and skill is negligence.[4]

When the attorney disobeys his client's instructions, he is responsible for ensuing loss,[5] as when he delays suit on a note placed in his hands for collection, with instructions to bring suit, and the maker subsequently becomes in-

---

1 Weeks on Attorneys, 284.
2 Pitt *v.* Yalden, 4 Burr. 2060.
3 Godfrey *v.* Dalton, 6 Bing. 460.
4 Holmes *v.* Peck, 1 R. I. 245.
5 Gilbert *v.* Williams, 8 Mass. 57.

solvent.[1] The client cannot, however, control the attorney in the due and orderly conduct of a suit, and the attorney should do what the court would order to be done, though the client instruct otherwise.[2]

The attorney does not guarantee that he will succeed in legal proceedings, or that his opinions are sound, or that he will be sustained by the higher courts.[3] He undertakes only to avoid errors which no member of his profession of ordinary prudence, dilligence and skill would commit.[4] If he commit an error in process or his papers are defective from lack of dilligence, he is liable.[5] The want of reasonable care and dilligence constitute gross negligence, for which he must be answerable.[6] The question of negligence is for the jury ;[7] the burden of proving negligence is on the plaintiff,[8]

---

[1] Cox v. Livingston, 2 W. & S. 103.

[2] Read v. French, 28 N. Y. 285.

[3] Weeks on Attorneys, § 290.

[4] Bowman v. Tallman, 27 How. Pr. 212.

[5] Dearborn v. Dearborn, 15 Mass. 316.

[6] Weeks on Attorneys, § 293.

[7] Rhines v. Evans, 66 Pa. St. 192; Hunter v. Caldwell, 10 Q. B. 69 ; Reece v. Rigley, 4 B. & A. 202.

[8] Wharton on Negligence, § 752.

and the measure of damages recoverable is the actual loss sustained by the client.[1]

Dealings with Client.

Bouvier states that the principal duties of an attorney are to be true to the court and to his client; to manage the business of his client with care, skill and integrity; to keep his client informed as to the state of his business; to keep his secrets confided to him as such, and that for a violation of his duties, an action will in general lie; and, in some cases, he may be punished by attachment. His services are to be justly compensated. The same author says that the duties of the client to his counsel are to give him written authority; to disclose his case with perfect candor; to offer spontaneously advances of money to his attorney; at the end of the suit to promptly pay his attorney his fees. He also defines the client's rights as follows: 1. To be dilligently served in the management of his business. 2. To be informed of its progress. 3. That his counsel will

1 Weeks on Attorneys, § 482.

not disclose what has been professionally confided to him.

The purchase by an attorney from his client during litigation of the subject matter of the action is held to be void.[1] If the attorney in a suit purchase the subject matter thereof, the client may usually set aside the same, unless the attorney show conclusively that no advantage was taken, that everything was explained to the client, and that the price was fair and reasonable.[2] The attorney must show that the client acted freely and understandingly.[3] The law does not prohibit him from purchasing from the client, but casts on him the burden of proving the justice and fairness of the whole transaction, and that the price paid was adequate.[4] The rule is that the attorney must make a full disclosure of every fact which might influence the decision of the client on the question of sale.[5] Courts of equity have,

[1] West v. Raymond, 21 Ind. 305.

[2] Valentine v. Stewart, 15 Calf. 387 ; Ford v. Harrington, 16 N. Y. 285; Mills v. Mills, 26 Conn. 213; Jennings v. McConnel, 17 Ill. 148.

[3] Brock v. Barnes, 40 Barb. (N. Y.) 521.

[4] Yeamans v. James, 27 Kan. 195.

[5] Rogers v. Marshall, 3 McCray (U. S.), 76.

on the ground of public policy, set aside gifts
by the client to the attorney made during the
period when the client had entrusted the management of his affairs to the attorney, although
no actual fraud was shown.[1]

Disbarment of Attorneys.

The statutes of Westminster (1 & 4 Hen.
IV., c. 18) expressly recognized the power and
jurisdiction of the court to summarily punish
or to suspend attorneys from practice, or to
strike them from the roll on the theory that
attorneys were considered as officers of the
court. The ground of the interference is the
dignity of the court offended in the conduct
of its officer, and its object is to punish miscon-
duct or disobedience and to reinstate the injured party in his rights.

The summary jurisdiction of the court over
attorneys has been held to extend to the following matters: Compelling an attorney to
perform his undertaking;[2] staying proceed-

1 Wells *v.* Middleton, 1 Cox, 112; Montesquieu *v.* Sandys,
1 Bach & B. 312.

2 Burrel *v.* Jones, 3 Barn. & A. 47; *Ex parte* Hughes, 5

ings begun without authority, on motion ;[1] compelling observance of good faith with clients;[2] preventing disclosure of confidential communications ; [3] compelling the delivery of papers which he has no right to retain ;[4] to punishment of contempt of court,[5] etc. The court will strike the name of an attorney from the rolls for malpractice, although it be not indictable.[6] The court has authority to suspend an attorney from practising for a limited time, or to expel him entirely ; and may, for that purpose, inquire in a summary manner as to any charges of malpractice alleged against him.[7] The act of the court in dismissing an attorney from the Bar for his conduct is not a criminal nor *quasi*-criminal proceeding, nor is the order a personal punishment, but a

---

Idem. 482; Iverson *v.* Corington, 1 Barn. & C. 160 ; Matter of H., 87 N. Y. 251.

[1] See Weeks on Attorneys, § 79.

[2] Weeks on Attorneys, § 77.

[3] People *v.* Barker, 56 Ill. 287.

[4] Weeks on Attorneys, §§ 92, 93.

[5] Weeks on Attorneys, § 97.

[6] U. S. *v.* Porter, 2 Cr. 60.

[7] *Ex parte* Burr, 2 Cr. 879.

mode of the court to get rid of an improper officer.[1]

To maintain a motion to strike from the rolls, the charge must affect the official character of the attorney,[2] and discreditable acts not connected with professionable duties, such as attempting to make opposing attorney drunk, will not give the court requisite jurisdiction.[3] Indulging in vices not affecting professional or personal integrity is not groundfor disbarment.[4]

[1] Bradley v. Fisher, 7 D. C. 82.

[2] Ex parte Steinman & Hensel, 95 Pa. St. 220; S. C., 40 Am. Rep. 637.

[3] Dicken's Case, 67 Pa. St. 169.

[4] Baker v. Commonwealth, 10 Bush (Ky.) 592.

EXTRACTS FROM ADDRESS

OF

HON. DANIEL S. DICKENSON, D LIVERED BE-
FORE THE GRADUATING CLASS OF LAW DE-
PARTMENT OF HAMILTON COLLEGE, CLINTON,
N. Y., JULY, 21, 1858.

"Among all the occupations of life, that of
the lawyer is the most laborious and responsible. It has been justly termed the noblest of
professions; but let no one enter upon it
reposing on the slovenly idea of 'masterly in-
activity,' or for the purpose of appearing upon
its parade days, or holiday occasions. He
must, if he would attain respectable eminence,
pass through an ordeal as severe as a furnace
seven times heated. He must be prepared to
hold intercourse with every variety of human
character, in its best as well as its most aban-
doned forms, and will need, to sustain him in
his extremity, the wisdom, meekness and patience of the patriarchs, and the learning of
Aristotle and a Paul.

"In the countless conflicts which arise from
the business transactions of every day life, in

all that disturbs the social or domestic relations, in matters relating to the rights of property by devise and inheritance, in every wrong,
direct or consequential, real or imaginary,
serious or trivial, the parties fly to him for
advice, friendly as well as professionally, and
invoke his assistance and consolation. He
must, at times, witness the exhibition of man's
worst passions — listening with becoming patience to the most tedious and frivolous relations, indulge the most unreasonable caprices,
and realize how fervent should be the petition
to be delivered 'from envy, hatred, and malice, and all uncharitableness;' and one of his
first and last, his earliest and latest duties, too,
requiring the exercise of all his wisdom and
firmness, will be to refuse, with stern and un-
yielding resolution, to commence prosecutions
upon the importunity of heated and exasper-
ated clients, where they have no just or substan-
tial cause.

"In his practice at the bar, he should remember that there is no place where good
manners and courteous demeanor appear to
better advantage, or command higher estimation. If his temper is occasionally tested, as

it will be, by an imperious and tyrannical judge, a vulgar opponent, or a false and obstinate witness, perfect self-possession and command will give him an incalculable advantage for the occasion, and illustrate then, as throughout his life, the inspired sentiment, that he that is slow to anger is better than the mighty, and he that ruleth his spirit, than he that taketh a city. His integrity should be uncompromising, his morals pure, his tastes refined, and his associations elevated. The influence of his example must be potent for good or for evil, and no social vice should stain his record, no debasing practices abridge his usefulness. He should studiously observe the conventional proprieties of society, and lead the way for those whose relations are less commanding, and whose opportunities are more limited.

"Within his professional sphere, he must strangle corruption, the first whisper it murmurs, before its pestilent taint is diffused throughout the atmosphere. He must trample upon fraud, extortion and oppression, wherever found, before they swell into rankness, and generate their Pandora brood of vassal vices.

He must take by the hand shrinking, trembling
innocence, and lead her forth vindicated by the
instinctive sympathies of law.   Where error
flaunts her banner, and her Cassandras croak
of evil, he must defy all augury, and wage a
war of extermination with weapons drawn
from the exhaustless armory of truth.   He
must learn to weild alternately the club of
Hercules, the battle-axe of Richard, and the
scimetar of Saladin, and bear in mind that the
wild rage of a strong Roderick may be foiled
by the steady skill of a cool, self-reliant Fitz-
James.   But in the battle of life the conflict
with himself should be the greatest; and when
that is nobly achieved, the victory is won.

"There is no royal road to position at the
bar; no stealthy by-way through which it can
be reached; no slippery and filthy step-stone
by which bribery can ascend to purchase it; no
hot-bed growth which will produce it; no forc-
ing process which will prove successful.   No
superficial gilding will conceal shameful ignorance; no spread-eagle declamation pass current as a substitute for knowledge; no spout-
ing and floundering on the surface deceive a
discerning public.   But drafts at sight upon

the golden granary of learning will always command a premium, and be duly honored.

" The lawyer should never bring a case into court without thorough and elaborate preparation. He must labor when courts indulge in relaxation, and study when his clients slumber. If he is deficient in elementary knowledge, or ignorant of the principles which govern his case, he is detected, the first sentence he utters, by the mature experience of the bench, the learning of the bar, the keen discernment of the jury, and the sympathetic common-sense of the tittering spectators ; and he is thereafter consigned, by universal consent, to that somewhat numerous class in the profession, who are more expensive to society in proportion to their numbers than any other, without being more ornamental, and stand or sit about the courts as statues at large."

* * * * * * * *

"Those who were good lawyers before the introduction of the Code conformed to its provisions with but little inconvenience, and were good lawyers still. Those who were admitted afterwards, but understood its objects and uses, and read thoroughly the elementary principles of their profession, in due time took respectable position at the bar.　But scores, unfitted by capacity, tact, and taste, deficient in the plainest rudiments of learning, destitute of general knowledge or education, forgetting that

"Honor and shame from no conditions rise,"

and captivated by the idea that the lawyer held an elevated and honorable rank in society, especially if he deserved it, learned like magpies to repeat the Code, and, under the unhealthy stimulus which it generated, shot up like a crop of mushrooms, in a single night as it were, and became full-fledged Code lawyers; leaving fertile acres untilled and the artisan's hammer reposing in the workshop, that the best might shortly wither by the wayside and betake themselves to other callings, and the worst strut as the rear guard of the profession and foster petty and demoralizing litigation.

" To understand the present system of practice, the lawyer must be incidentally familiar with the Code.　But he may commit it entirely to memory, including its latest, not to say greenest, crop of amendments, and be no lawyer, without the learning which a long course of general elementary reading and severe mental discipline alone can give him. If early advantages have been denied him, it is no apology for ignorance ; but he must improve with increased dilligence those within his reach at a later period. So far as true legal learning is concerned, the student might as well read the by-laws of a bank, the ordinances of a village, the regulations of a gas company, or the constitution of a sewing society, as the Code ; for neither will give him any idea whatever of legal science.

"The proper course of elementary reading has been so often and accurately indicated in the course of your instruction in this excellent institution, that you need not to be reminded of Bracton and Fleta, of Ulpain, Coke and Blackstone, or of Kent and Cruise and Story ; but you may be profitably reminded that mere reading, unaccompanied with a clear and comprehensive understanding, will be of little service, and that it is better to read little which is thoroughly understood than much which is left undigested.

"No dilligent student, of good natural capacity, ever failed of success — no indolent genius,

however gifted and brilliant, ever gained eminence at the bar. By reading, you gather the
best thoughts of the noblest minds for genera-
tions — you bask in the light of all the learning from the earliest dawn of civilization—you
select your weapons of moral warfare from the
world's mighty armory, and if they are well
chosen, woe be to him who encounters you
unprepared.

"But mere legal reading will not suffice.
The lawyer should be well versed in history,
ancient and modern, and know where Sappho
sung, where Solon legislated and Homer
chanted his triumphs ; in philosophy, natural,
mental, and moral ; in medical jurisprudence ;
in a general knowledge of the mechanical arts ;
in the regulations and usages of trade, commerce, banking, and finance, and in other pursuits, callings, and professions. In short, he
must so accustom his mind to investigation that
he can, as if by intuition, grasp any subject
presented for his consideration, and master its
details and explain its intricacies.

"The lawyer is accustomed to lead in legislative and other public assemblies, and should
be versed in the recondite science of solving

social problems, termed political economy ; and especially in these days of constitution making, mending, and breaking, he should be familiar with the true theories of free government, and contribute the influence of his precept and example to inculcate principles which will diffuse prosperity, contentment, and happiness, and discourage restlessness, ignoble office-seeking ambition, and indolence among the masses.

"One of the prevailing errors, not to say curses, of the times is the belief that 'the post of honor is a private station' no longer — that the ordinary industrial pursuits of life are too tame and spiritless for the times, if not actually discreditable; and hence office-seeking comes up, like the plagues of Egypt, into the very beds and boards and kneading-troughs, and all classes, in a greater or less degree, are afflicted by the contagion. So desirable has office become, that those who fail to obtain one incorporal in character content themselves with a material substitute. The merchant no longer seeks his counting-room to strike his balances, but makes his computations in his office; the clergyman has forsaken his study as too old-fashioned for the age, and muses upon the beauties of redeeming grace and dying love in his office ; the physician administers his scruples and the hotel keeper his drams from their respective offices, and the proprietor of the livery stable sits complacently and securely in an office of greater stability than all the others.

* * * * * * * *

"In choosing the profession of law, you go out into the world like the knights of chivalry, to espouse the cause of justice and innocence, and to stand between oppression and its victims. Armed with the panoply of learning and protected by social virtues, though unknown in the lists, you may fearlessly enter and strike with the pointed end of your spear the shields of the Brian Du Bois Gilberts.

" The march of time is onward, like the flow of an unremitting stream. One generation succeeds another, like the waves that roll over the surface of the deep. Those who now fill the responsible trusts in the various departments of life will soon all be laid in the dust. Soon you must be called to plead at the Bar, to declare decisions from the Bench, and to stand as representatives in the Legislative Forum. Fear not, falter not ; let your course be upward and onward, and length of days shall be in your right hand, and in your lelt riches and honor.

"Expect not to commence in your professional career where eminent experience leaves off, but strive to emulate the noble example of him whose munificence endowed this fountain of legal light and learning, for the diffusion of a science at whose shrine he had worshipped with an eastern devotion, and the elevation and refinement of a profession that he loved — the lamented Maynard. Contemplate his progress, from humble beginnings, through a course of toil, of severe application, of self-denial as a student, to the ripe and accomplished scholar, the respected and virtuous citizen, the profound lawyer, and the wise judge and statesman ; when in the maturity of his strength and the zenith of his fame, too strong for earthly courts, he passed away to a tribunal,

> ' Where every right decree is ratified,
> And every wrong reversed and set aside.'

'Tread lightly upon his ashes, ye men of genius, for he was your kinsman.' Cherish his memory with veneration, and cast chaplets upon his tomb. .

"The history of the Bar is a history of illus-
trious examples, patriotic impulses, and noble
deeds. Its members have been conspicuous
among those who have at all times shed lustre
upon our country's fame ; they led our armies
in the fearful days of revolutionary peril, and
gave to the cause of liberty a declaration of the
rights of man which will throw light along the
shadowy path of tradition when records shall
exist no longer, and every page of history
shall have faded away.

"The noble intellects of a country are the
sheet-anchor of its hope; they protect its moral
as the citizen soldiery do its material outposts.
In the ebbs and flows of life's mighty ocean ;
amidst the storms which agitate its bosom and
heave it in maddening, whirling currents now
riding mountain high, now yawning in fearful
chasms, now placid and serene—no impotent
Xerxes with his paper constitutions can bind it
in fetters, nor Canute with his penal statutes
limit the swelling of its waves. The stream cannot be raised higher nor made more pure than the
fountain, nor the constitution of laws of a State
excel in strength or wisdom the great body of
its people. Laws may punish vice, but it is

not their office to force the growth of virtue.
The security of a State rests in the sound morality and intelligence of those who compose
it; and when these safeguards fail, the prob-
lem of self-government will be finally solved,
for paper laws will prove a delusive mockery.
No standing armies, no bristling bayonet, no
naval armaments can quicken the pulsations of
liberty or measure the heart-throbs of emanci-
pated man.   Religion, virtue, intelligence,
point the pathway of duty and assure us of the
rewards which await their votaries.   During
the last century, an eminent lawyer of the Old
World, by the feeble and flickering light of
liberty which forced its way through the cracks
and crannies of a stultified system of monarchy,
caught up the true inspiration, and by pregnant interrogatory and answer (which, though
worn with time and service, are always new),
well declared the true principles of a government of laws :

        " ' What constitutes a State?
Not high-raised battlement or labored mound,
    Thick wall or moated gate ;
Not cities proud, with spires and turrets crowned ;
    Not huge and broad armed ports,
Where, laughing at the storm, rich navies ride ;

Not starred and spangled courts,
Where low-browed baseness wafts perfume to pride.
   No! Men—high-minded Men,
With powers as far above dull brutes endued,
   In forest, brake, or den,
As beasts excel cold brakes or brambles rude;
   Men, who their duties know,
But know their rights, and knowing dare maintain,
   Prevent the long-aimed blow,
And crush the tyrant while they rend the chain,
   These constitute a State:
And sovereign law, that State's collected will,
   O'er thrones and globes elate,
Sits empress, crowning good, repressing ill.' "

INDEX.

A.

B.

(93)

G.

H.

I.

J.

K.